3/97

CHANUTE PUBLIC LIBRARY
111 North Lincoln
CHANUTE, KS 66720

Life of the Ant

CHANUTE PUBLIC LIBRARY
111 North Lincoln
CHANUTE, KS 66720

First Steck-Vaughn Edition 1992

This book has been reviewed
for accuracy by
Walter L. Gojmerac
Professor of Entomology
University of Wisconsin—Madison.

Library of Congress Cataloging in Publication Data

Nanao, Jun.
   Life of the ant.

   (Nature close-ups)
   Translation of: Ari no ichinichi / text by Jun
Nanao, photographs by Satoshi Kuribayashi.
   Summary: Discusses the life cycle, behavior patterns,
and habitats of various species of ants.
   1. Ants—Juvenile literature. [1. Ants]
I. Kuribayashi, Satoshi, 1939-   ill. II. Title.
III. Series.
QL568.F7N36   1986   595.79′6   85-28198

ISBN 0-8172-2539-0 (lib. bdg.)
ISBN 0-8172-2564-1 (softcover)

This edition first published in 1986 by Raintree Publishers Inc.,
a Division of Steck-Vaughn Company.

Text copyright © 1986 by Raintree Publishers Inc., translated from *The Daily Life of the Ant* copyright © 1973 by Jun Nanao.

Photographs copyright © 1973 by Satoshi Kuribayashi.

World English translation rights for *Color Photo Books on Nature* arranged with Kaisei-Sha through Japan Foreign-Rights Center.

All rights reserved. No part of the material protected by this copyright may be reproduced or utilized in any form by any means, electronic or mechanical, including photocopying, recording, or by any information storage and retrieval system, without permission in writing from Steck-Vaughn Company, P.O. Box 26015, Austin, TX 78755. Printed in the United States of America.

   2 3 4 5 6 7 8 9 0   95 94 93 92 91

Life of the Ant

RAINTREE
STECK-VAUGHN
LIBRARY
A Division of Steck-Vaughn Company

Ants are everywhere—in fields and gardens, along country roads, and on city sidewalks. There are more than ten thousand different kinds, or species, of ants in the world. They are found everywhere except in the coldest climates.

Ants are social insects. That means they live together in groups and depend on one another to perform various roles. Groups of ants are called colonies.

The only duty of the male ants is to mate with the queens. The life-long job of the queen is to lay eggs. The worker ants clean the nest, care for the queen and the young ants, and build and defend the nest.

Because ants are social creatures, they often work together to bring food to the nest. To find their way back to the nest, they use their long feelers, or antennae, to follow the scent of fellow worker ants.

◀ **A black ant coming out of its nest.**
This worker ant sticks its head out of the nest and uses its antennae to sniff the air for danger.

▶ **A line of black carpenter ants.**
These ants are following the trails left by others from the same nest as they search for food.

▲ Black carpenter ants collecting the pollen from a camellia flower.

▲ Black ants licking the nectar from a camomile flower.

Ants eat many different kinds of food, depending on the species. Some hunt, or prey upon, other insects. Many drink sweet flower nectar and plant juices.

Most ants have two compound eyes which are made up of about one thousand tiny eyes. Some ants also have three simple eyes. Even so, not all ants can see well. So they rely on their antennae to smell and touch objects. When an ant has found flower nectar by sniffing it, it sticks its head down into the flower petals and licks up the nectar.

An ant's stomach has two parts. One part digests the food the ant eats. The other part is called the crop. In the crop, the ant can store food to be eaten later. When its crop is full of nectar, the ant drags its heavy body back to the nest. It shares the nectar in its crop with other hungry worker ants and with developing ants, called larvae.

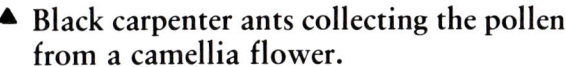

◀ This black ant buries its head deep in the flower petals as it licks the nectar.

▲ If an ant wants some nectar from another ant, it goes up to it and taps it with its antennae.

Ants use their antennae in special ways to communicate with one another. They "talk" by touching each other's antennae. The ants' antennae are jointed, so they bend and move easily in many directions. An ant detects sounds and odors by waving its feelers in the air. Ants also feel their way along by tapping the ground, or other objects, with their antennae.

If an ant is hungry and cannot find any food itself, it may tap another worker with its antennae. This is a signal that it wants some of the food stored in the other ant's crop. The ant with food will bring up, or regurgitate, some of the nectar from its crop and pass it to the hungry ant.

◄ This black carpenter ant is sharing the nectar from its crop with another ant.

Ants are social insects and rely on one another to keep the colony thriving. But from time to time ants fight among themselves, usually over food.

However, ants are much more likely to fight with members of other colonies. Two colonies may fight one another over food. Or they may fight simply because their nests are too close together. All the ants from one colony have a particular odor. So one ant can recognize another from the same colony by its smell.

In some species, soldier ants help other worker ants to defend the nest. Soldier ants are the biggest and strongest of the workers, and they have jaws designed for biting.

When an ant colony is invaded by enemies, soldier ants signal to other workers for help by releasing a special chemical substance. The other ants rush to the rescue in a massive team effort to defend the nest.

◀ This soldier red ant and other workers are attacking an enemy black ant.

◄ Black ants tap aphids with their antennae and collect honeydew.

▶ This ladybug is a predator of aphids.

All species of ants seem to be fond of a sweet liquid that comes from aphids. In fact, because of their fondness for this honeydew, there is a special helping relationship between ants and aphids.

Aphids feed on plants by sucking sap from them. When the ants gather around the aphids and tap or stroke them on the back with their antennae, the aphids excrete honeydew from their abdomens and the ants lick it up.

The ants, in turn, guard the aphids from insect predators such as ladybugs and lacewings. Some species of ants are so fond of honeydew that they take aphid eggs into their own nest and care for them during the winter. When the baby aphids hatch in the spring, the ants carry them back to their favorite plants. By taking care of the aphids in this way, the ants are guaranteed of always having a supply of honeydew.

Hidden inside this fluffy white substance that looks like cotton is a relative of the aphid—a scale insect. Its white covering protects it and keeps it hidden from enemies.

A long tube curves from the back of the scale insect and extends outside the protective covering. From the end of the tube, honeydew is excreted. When the ant strokes the tube with its antennae, the scale insect excretes drops of the sweet liquid. The worker ant gathers large drops of the honeydew in its jaws and carries them off.

The ant guards the scale insect, as it does aphids, by chasing off ladybugs and other predators.

● Ants collecting the sweet liquid produced by the scale insect. They carry the juice in their jaws.

Many species of ants build complex underground nests with many rooms and tunnels. There are rooms for storing food, nurseries for the eggs and larvae, and a special room for the queen ant.

But some species do not build much of a nest at all. They settle for a makeshift one, under a stone or beneath a piece of wood. If it rains and the nest becomes flooded, the ants must move to another place.

Then the ants form a long line and go on the march, in search of a good site for a new nest. They carry a precious cargo in their mouths— the eggs, larvae, and pupae of the developing ants in the colony.

◀ Ants carrying larvae and eggs, moving to a new nest.

▲ A black ant and a butterfly eating watermelon.

In some species of ants, like the harvester ants, the workers each search for food on their own. In other species, certain workers leave the nest to scout around. When they find a large piece of food, they rush back to the nest to share the news with fellow workers. They communicate their discovery to the other workers by tapping them with their antennae.

The workers respond. Soon, a two-way line is formed between the nest and the food. The ants hurry along the trail, guided by the scent of other ants.

▲ Black carpenter ants sharing a piece of candy they have found on the ground.

Ants love sweet, juicy things like watermelon and candy. They quickly find their way to any sweet food, even if it is inside houses or on picnic tables. Eating a piece of hard candy is a large task for a small ant. It may take two or three days of steady chewing and swallowing, bit by bit, before the ant manages to eat the entire piece.

▲ A black ant dragging the dead body of a bug back to its nest.

Certain types of ants are predators. They kill and eat other insects. Army ants are among the fiercest of these hunters. They prey upon spiders, insects, and even slow-moving animals. Often soldier ants, with their strong jaws, will join the other workers in the colony in attacking large insect prey. Some soldier ants sting their prey. Others bite their victims and then spray them with a poison which paralyzes them. Then the dead insect is dragged back to the nest so other ants can share the food. Or, the victim may be torn to pieces and carried bit by bit back to the underground nest.

▲ A black ant struggling to retrieve a bird's feather.

Ants carry all sorts of things. They can carry things up to fifty times their own size. The ant in the photo above struggles with a bird's feather. If it manages to drag it back to the nest, the feather may serve two purposes. If it still has flesh particles attached to it, the ants in the colony will feed on it. And the remaining soft plumes may be used to line the nest.

▲ These ants work together to carry a seed back to the nest.

Harvester ants are very busy in the autumn. They collect seeds and berries and store them in the nest for food during the long winter. Each ant searches for seeds on its own. It then drags its heavy load back to the nest, where the seeds are stored in special chambers. A certain kind of acid inside the nest prevents the seeds and berries from rotting. The heat and moisture in the nest changes the starch in the seeds to sugar, which the ants can eat.

Some kinds of harvester ants may even take the seeds outside to dry them in the sun. This also helps to change the starch to sugar. All members of the colony eat the stored berries and seeds. Worker ants take off the hard outer casing of the seeds and berries and feed the queen and larvae the soft inner part.

◀ The ants choose the largest seeds and berries they can find.

▶ Seeds stored inside an ant's nest.

After a queen ant mates, she usually begins a new colony on her own. Using her jaws and claws, she digs a small hole in the ground. Then she seals the entrance to her nest and lays her tiny white eggs and cares for them.

When the eggs hatch, worm-like larvae emerge. They are blind and helpless and cannot move. The queen cleans and feeds them. In about a month, the larvae shed their skins and become pupae. Some species spin protective coverings, or cocoons, at this stage. Other pupae lie on their backs, naked and helpless, nurtured by the queen. The pupal stage may last two or three weeks, during which time the body of the adult ant is slowly forming. Because ants go through such drastic physical changes, they are said to experience a metamorphosis. Many other insects go through the same stages of development: egg, larva, pupa, and adult.

As soon as the new workers emerge as adults, the queen's long job is over. From now on, her only duty will be to lay more eggs. The new workers will do all the necessary chores for the colony. They search for food, build and guard the nest, and care for the young.

▼ The big ant in the middle is the queen ant.

▼ These worker ants are looking after the pupae.

Let's Find Out

Where Do Ants Build Their Nests?

Each species of ant makes its own kind of nest. Some ants build underground nests. You can tell where these nests are because there is usually a little mound of loose dirt around the entrance leading underground. Some ants live under the bark of dead trees. If you see a steady stream of ants going into a hole in an old tree, that's a good clue that ants live there.

Although the shapes and locations of nests may vary, they have one thing in common. Each nest has many rooms. There are rooms for keeping the larvae and pupae. There are rooms for storing food. And there is a room where the queen lays her eggs.

Some colonies have millions of ants. The ants spend a lot of time making sure the entrances and exits of the nest are clear of leaves and dead twigs.

An ant's nest in a hollow tree.

Pupae in a nest. They are in cocoons which keep them safe.

A black carpenter ant is busy building a nest.

A nest in a mound of grass.

A nest in a hollow stem.

Black carpenter ants are very careful to make at least two entrances to a nest. If one of the entrances becomes blocked, the ants can get out of the nest through the other entrance.

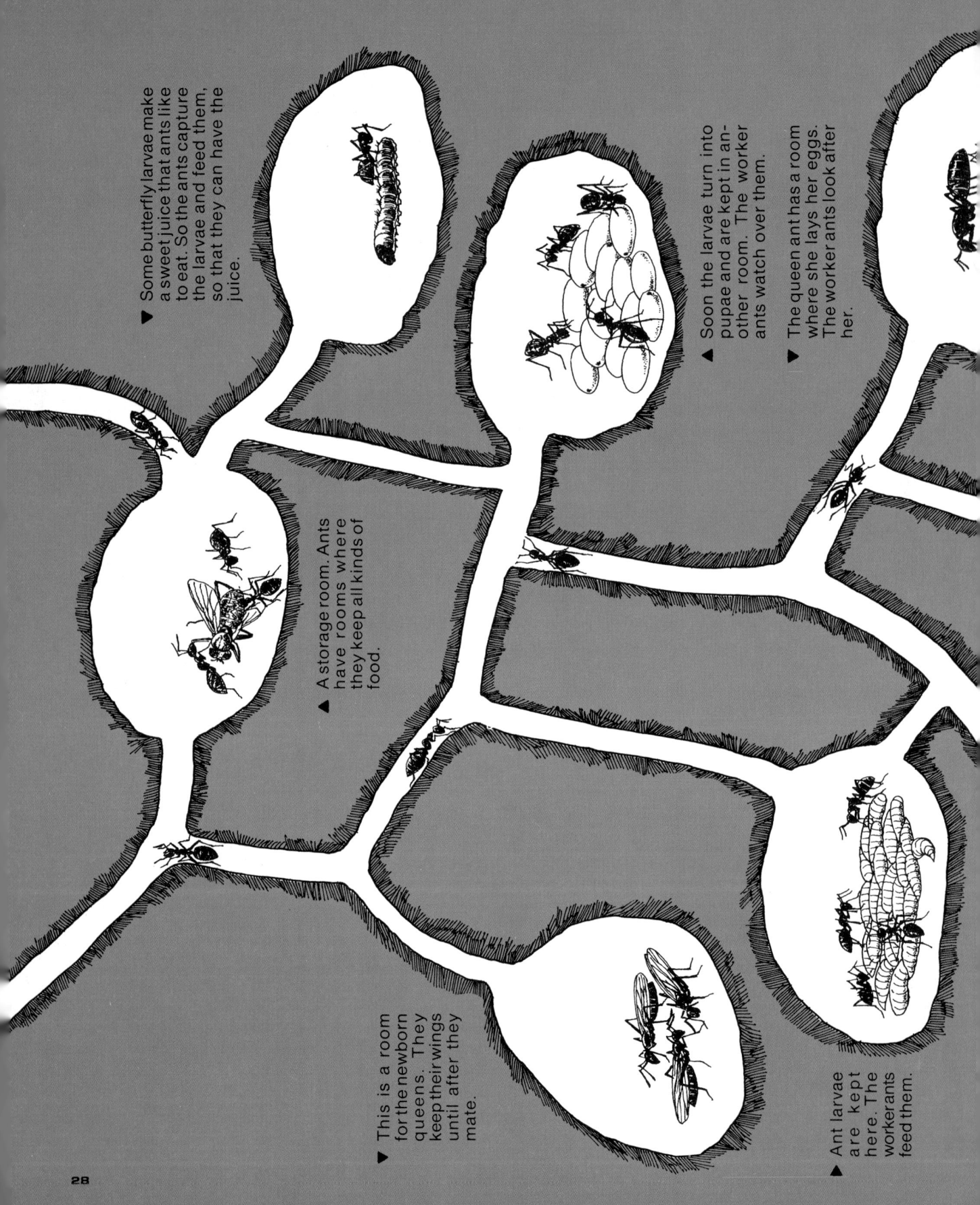

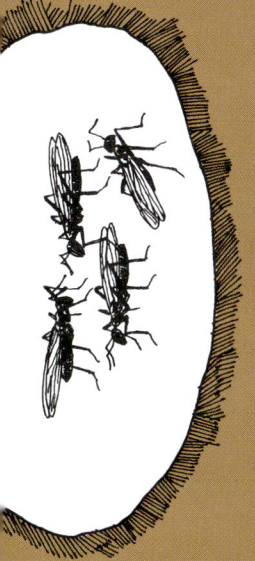

▶ The male ants' room. Their only job is to mate with the queens from other colonies. The worker ants look after them, too.

▶ Worker ants fighting.

▶ A queen ant and her eggs.

▶ The nest entrance has been broken. Worker ants repair it.

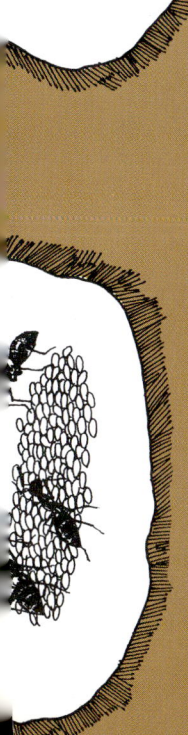

▶ Here the worker ants look after the eggs until the larvae emerge.

▶ Worker ants look after butterfly larvae.

▶ Worker ants look after the queen, her eggs, larvae, and pupae.

29

Let's Find Out

How Do Ants Carry So Much Nectar?

▼ A black carpenter ant licking the nectar of an azalea.

A worker ant has two parts to its stomach. One part digests food. The other part, which is called the crop, stores food for the other ants in the nest. The worker ant stores the nectar that it collects from flowers, along with honeydew from aphids, in this crop. When its crop is full, the ant returns to the nest and feeds the larvae and the other ants by bringing up food from its crop and passing it on to others.

▼ The large jaws of a black carpenter ant. The jaws are called mandibles.

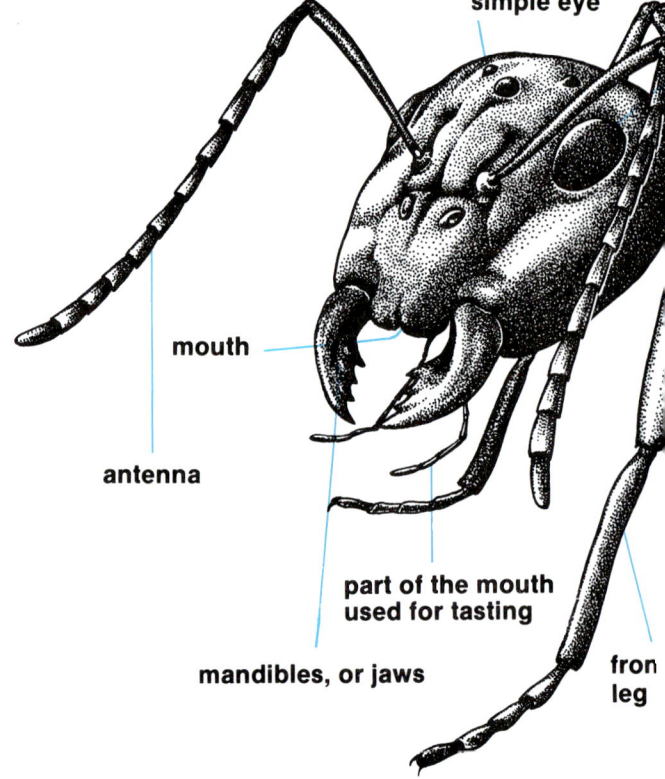

The part of the ant's stomach nearest the head is called the crop. This is where it stores the food which it will pass on to other ants. When it wants to feed itself, it opens the valves between the crop and its own stomach to let the food pass through the tubes.

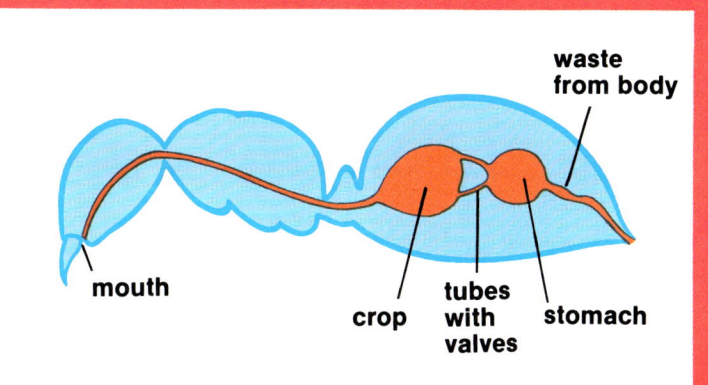

The petiole is very narrow. It lets the ant bend in many different directions.

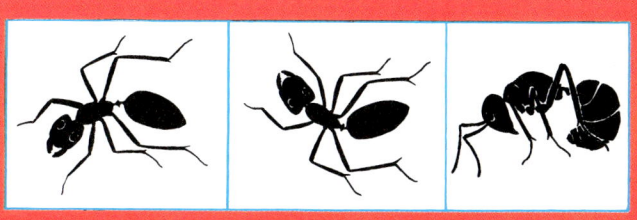

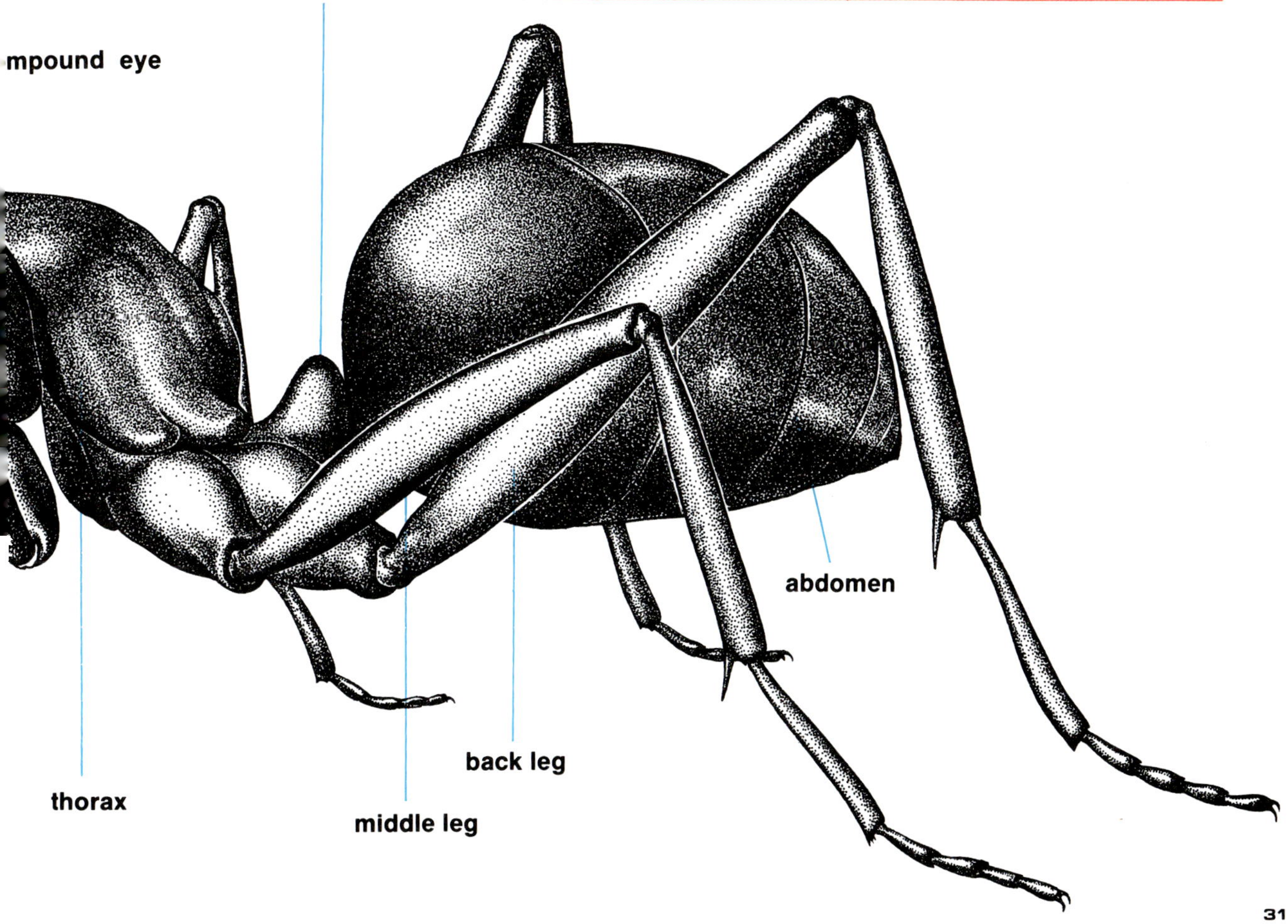

GLOSSARY

abdomen—the rear section of an insect's body. (p. 13)

antennae—the movable feelers on an insect's head, which detect odor and movement. (pp. 5, 7, 9)

colonies—large groups of insects that live together and depend on each other for survival, such as ants and some bees. (pp. 5, 11, 17)

crop—a special storage area for food. Both bees and ants have crops. (pp. 7, 9, 30)

honeydew—a sweet substance excreted by aphids. (pp. 13, 15, 30)

metamorphosis—a process of development during which physical changes take place. Complete metamorphosis involves four stages: egg, larva, pupa, and adult. Incomplete metamorphosis occurs in three stages: egg, nymph, and adult. (p. 24)

predators—animals that hunt or kill other animals for food. (pp. 13, 15, 20)

prey—animals that are killed by predators. (p. 20)

social insects—insects that live together and depend on each other for survival. Social insects live in large groups called colonies. (pp. 5, 11)

species—a group of animals which scientists have identified as having common traits. (pp. 5, 7, 13)